Contents

Introduction

POLICE JOKES MIX

POLICE JOKES THAT COULD GET ARRESTED LAUGHTER

REDDIT POLICE JOKES

PUNS AND JOKES BY POLICE ARE SO FUNNY

JOKES WITH A POLICE OFFICER

CRAZY COPS JOKE

KNOCK-KNOCK POLICE JOKES

POLICE HUMOR FOR KIDS

## INTRODUCTION:

In this book you will find exactly what you have been looking for a long time. Here the most beautiful and funniest jokes, puns and joke riddles about policemen and everyday police life are combined with each other and summarized in a unique collection.

Of course, policemen and the police everyday life are afflicted with many clichés and that is of course what this book is about. Nevertheless, it should never be ignored that police officers are faced with new challenges every working day and what they accomplish. They are an essential part of making us feel safe. And as you will see in this book, they manage to make us happy not only with their deeds but also with jokes.

So now enough of the preface, have fun reading, browsing and laughing :)

# Police Jokes Mix:

1.

My wife dressed as an attractive police officer and detained me on the grounds that I was an excellent bed partner. I was cleared of all charges following a brief trial.

2.

"I was stopped by a policeman, who asked for my papers. "Scissors, I win," I said before accelerating. Given that he has been after me for the past 45 minutes, he must have sought a rematch."

3.

Policeman: "I'm arresting you for downloading the entirety of Wikipedia illegally."

Wait, I can explain everything, said the man.

4.

A drunken man is stumbling around the city. When the man approaches an officer to report that his automobile was stolen.

Where were you when you last saw it, the policeman queries?

"It was just here at the end of this key," the inebriated person claims.

Well, I advise you get over to the station house and fill out a report, the police officer adds.

When the policeman remarks, "Hey, before you go, you might want to zip your fly," the alcoholic began to back away.

The inebriated man exclaims, "Aw, dude, they got my daughter, too," as he glances down.

5.

Why did the officer go the restroom? To do his duties.

6.

A drunk wakes up in jail, "Why am I here officer?"

"For drinking." replies the officer.

"Great," says the man. "When do we start?"

7.

Police Officer: "You're driving on the wrong side of the road." Driver: "Sorry, I'm English."

Police officer: (shouting) "Oii! It's the wrong said of the road he was driving down, innit?"

8.

An officer observes a woman standing in the middle of the street.

He approaches her and asks, "Are you OK?"

The woman replies, "Yes, but how do I get to the hospital?"

The officer says, "Just keep standing there."

9.

Why was the artist upset? She was being framed for murder!

10.

I'm issuing you a ticket for driving alone in the carpool lane, so there, police officer.

When you peek through my trunk, you'll feel foolish, I promise.

11.

"Usually, when they find out I have a record, police are astonished. However, I adore their biggest hits.

12.

While driving together, Heisenberg and Schrodinger are stopped by a police officer.

Did you realize you were traveling at 75 mph, the officer queries?

Oh crap, we're lost, Heisenberg sighs.

Unhappy, the officer opens the trunk and looks inside. And why is there a dead cat inside, he queries. There is now, Schrodinger grumbles.

13. " "I received a call from the police station requesting an interview. Funny... I don't recall submitting a job application there."

14.

A Nintendo police vehicle makes what noises?

Wiiu, Wiiu, Wiiu...

15.

Why was the skeleton taken into custody by the policeman?

The joint of his hand was visible to them.

16.

When the man was stopped, his vaporizer was in the cup holder. "You know, the news says those things are killing people," the officer remarked.

They're saying the same thing about you folks, the man chuckled.

He didn't chuckle.

17.

So this morning, a policeman knocked on my door. We think your dog has been after a youngster on a bike up the road, sir, he enquired. "Sorry officer, you may have the incorrect house," I said. My dog is not a bike owner."

18.

You have crimson eyes "the policeman stated. Have you been using marijuana?

I said, "Your eyes appear hazy. Have you eaten any doughnuts lately?

19. While on the motorway, a police officer sees an elderly woman crocheting while holding the steering wheel steady on her knees. He comes up next to the elderly woman and yells aggressively, "Pull over!" No, it's a scarf, the grandmother responds loudly.

20.

Why were police officers on the sand? A criminal wave was under suspicion!

21.

We are referred to as vital because it would be too honest to market us as scarified.

22.

We can complete this task quickly.

...or whichever United Airlines decides.

23.

Are you a police officer?

No, I'm an undercover investigator, said the officer.

"So, why are you in uniform?" said a tourist.

Officer: "I have the day off today."

24.

There is a guy in the community who is robbing police cars of their wheels. The cops are making every effort to apprehend him.

25.

Why do police people make such great volleyball players?

Because they understand how to protect and serve.

26.

I won't say anything without my lawyer present, a man in a questioning space asserts.

Officers: "You are the attorney."

That being said, where is my present?

27.

One foot was on the curb and the other was in the gutter as the man stumbled along the street.

When a policeman arrived, he said, "I must take you in, buddy. You're wasted."

Are you certain I'm drunk, officer? The drunken guy enquired.

The policeman said, "Yeah buddy, I'm sure, let's go."

The wino exhaled a breath of relief and exclaimed, "Thanks be to God. I believed I was paralyzed."

28.

If I were a police officer, I would issue tickets to those for failing to use their turn signals, both left and right.

29.

Policeman 1: "This murder looks to have ethnic undertones."

Officer 2 of the police: "Hate crime?"

Policeman one: "I detest crime, of sure. That is why I work as an officer."

30.

What distinguishes a police officer from a computer?

Troubleshooting is one.

## POLICE JOKES THAT COULD GET ARRESTED LAUGHTER:

1.

"A police officer with Alzheimer's disease stopped me. Upon approaching my window, he inquires, "Do I know why I pulled you over?""

2.

What do you name the act of taking a prisoner's mug shot? The selfie

3.

What did the police officer say to his navel?

You're wearing a vest. I'm happy to meet you!

4

A man who is obviously drunk is discovered by an officer.

We'll have to administer a drug test to you, he informs the man.

The man responds, "Cool, what drugs are we testing?" without any hesitation.

5.

Johnny threw the clock out the window, but why?

He wanted to see the passage of time!

6.

What are the officers' recommended meal groups?

Powdered, glazed, chocolate-frosted, and jelly.

7.

What did the police officer say to his navel?

You are wearing a vest!

8.

What is a fake noodle known as? The impasto

9.

What was spoken to the snowman by the policeman? Freeze!

10.

I imagine that the squad car officer is to the bike officer what a sketch artist is to an etch-a-sketch operator.

11.

Because L.A. is so hazardous, I have a pistol in my car. If the cops stop me, I can defend myself until the press arrives.

12.

What communication occurred between the two toilets?

You appear flushed.

13.

How did the hacker elude capture by the authorities? It was ransom ware.

14.

"If I continued to crack poor jokes, the cops threatened to arrest me. I stopped because I was afraid I would get locked up."

15.

"Police in my town detained a mime who had broken his left hand in a bar brawl. He still has the option to keep quiet."

16

At Tesla's robotics lab, there was a reported break-in, so police were called. Optimus committed the crime.

17.

A miner is stopped by a police officer for speeding on the highway.

"Who's automobile is this?" said the policeman. What's your destination? What are you doing?

Miners: "Mine."

18.

Today, my brother was killed.

Do you mind identifying the body? I must tell you that it was sliced up, the officer said.

"Yes, that's my brother Reese," I said.

Officer: "Are you sure? "Those are Reese's Pieces," I said.

19.

A blonde phones the police after accidently killing a policeman:

Greetings, is this 911? Yes, tell me about your emergency.

"I called to let you know that you are now 910," I said.

20.

" "I was recently stopped by a police officer. He approached, and I reached for my 9mm. He began writing me up for indecent exposure once he stopped laughing."

21.

An Irish priest gets stopped by a police officer while driving along a rural road. He finds an empty wine bottle in the car and detects alcohol on the priest's breath right away.

"Have you been drinking?" he asks. Just water, the priest says.

"Then why do I smell wine?" the cop asks in response.

The priest says as he examines the bottle: "Oh, my God! He's done it once more!"

22.

In the carpool lane, the man was stopped. Where's your passenger, policeman?

Man: "They're in the car behind me because of social distance."

23.

A Spanish photon was stopped by a police officer.

Do you know how fast you were traveling, the cop inquired?

"C," the photon signaled.

24.

"I used to sell beds for a living. One day, this guy entered and began getting into the beds while asking incredibly detailed questions. Then it dawned on me— he was a police officer working undercover."

25.

One Saturday night, a college professor is driving home while intoxicated. When the police stop him. "Excuse me, sir, you were speeding, you jumped a red light, and you look to be inebriated. Where are you going?" the policeman says as he approaches his window.

I am now my route to a lecture about the risks of using tobacco, drinking alcohol, and staying up late, the lecturer responds.

Who could be giving that type of talk at this hour, the policeman asks.

My wife," the professor replies.

26.

"I informed the policeman I had contacts when he pointed out that I should be wearing spectacles after looking at my driver's license. He didn't care who I knew, though, and still issued me a ticket.

27.

A police officer who doesn't get out of bed is what?

A cop working cover.

28.

A father is accompanying his son to purchase his first automobile. At one of the properties, the son notices an old, used police vehicle. "Dad! I desire that! That would be awesome! Can I use the police vehicle for a test drive? "No, son," the father responds. I demand that your automobile have functional turn signals and a reliable speedometer.

29.

A female driver is stopped. She attempts flirting with the officer as he walks to her car in an effort to avoid getting a ticket. She says, seductively, "Hello." He answers, "Hello. "I thought you didn't sell tickets to attractive women?" She cries. "We don't, and you're correct. Have a good day, and here is your ticket."

30.

The policeman stops the guy in his car. Officer of the law "You appear to have consumed alcohol. Could you please say the letters beginning with "M"?"

Guy: "No issue. Alphabet."

31.

What do attorneys put on for court? Lawsuits!

32.

When I spotted you driving down the road, the policeman said, "I figured you were at least 55."

Driver: "Officer, you're mistaken. I only appear that elderly because of my headgear.

33.

I questioned a new officer about what he would do if he had to detain his mother.

I'd call for backup, he declared.

34.

A speeder is stopped by a police officer. The officer inquires, "Do you know how fast you were going." The man responds, "130 km/h." Policeman astonished that the man admitted to speeding says, "Why were you driving 30 above the limit?" "I was navigating the traffic!" The policeman scans both sides of the street. "No other automobiles are here," The guy acknowledges, "I know, that's how far behind I am!

35.

Why wouldn't the shrimp distribute his loot?

Considering that he was a little shrimp

36.

What causes a soccer stadium to glow?

A game of soccer

37.

Why was it impossible for the police to inform the slain baker's family?

A John Dough, he was.

38.

What's dark and always found in a police car's trunk? The chair.

39.

How many police are required to install a light bulb?

Eleven, one to change the bulb. 10 to do the paperwork

40.

Policeman: "I'll follow you to the closest police station." 40

"What for?" I ask. I've forgotten the route, policeman.

41.

"The cops advised me to prepare for the worst one week after my wife went missing. I then returned to the charity shop and took all of her old clothing."

42.

"I enjoy their best hits, but the police are generally startled that I have a record!"

43.

Have you heard that the energizer bunny was taken into custody?

He was battery-charged.

44.

Do you aware your brother dropped out of the car a few miles back? Asked a state trooper who had stopped a farmer on a country road.

45.

In a car with a football player, an undocumented immigrant, and a Muslim, who is the driver?

Officer of the law

46.

A female police officer who plays the guitar is referred to as what?

RIFF SHE

47.

What do you call a police officer who is keeping an eye on cows?

Steak night!

48.

What do you call an escaped jail midget clairvoyant?

A tiny, medium-sized thing.

49.

Where do police officers go?

Helicopter police word! Interviewing the suspects was going on!

50.

Why was the cheetah detained by the police?

For exceeding the posted speed limit!

51.

Police just charged one man with battery theft and released another after they were caught stealing pyrotechnics!

52.

Yesterday, a guy was detained for pretending to be a helium balloon. After holding him for a bit, the cops released him.

53.

Tonight, the cops showed up at the man's home with a photo of his wife. Is this your wife, sir?

They questioned. The man, startled, said, "Yes." I'm afraid it appears like she was struck by a bus, they stated. I know, but she has a great personality, the man remarked.

54.

What distinguishes a police officer from a velociraptor?

Velociraptor can operate door handles.

55.

The passing of a former police officer. At the burial, the police chief spoke and wished the deceased "may he arrest in peace."

56.

A police you were approaching me quickly. I was making an effort to follow traffic.

No cops are present.

That is how far behind I am, I am aware.

57.

"My Tesla was taken! I reported an Edison when I phoned the police."

58.

"In a contest, I took home an iPhone 14. The phone's owner and police officers are the other two rivals."

59.

When I rolled down my window to ask what was wrong after a female cop pulled me over, she said, "NOTHING."

When Zia-infected mosquitoes attack, who do you call?

The SWAT group.

60.

A policeman pulled over a man for speeding.

Do you realize how fast you were moving, he asked? He answered, "I was trying to keep up with traffic.

There is no traffic, he declared.

That's how far behind I am, the man said.

61.

How many Karens are required to replace one light bulb?

Just one... to officer 911 and request that an officer respond to the menacing darkness.62.

62.

The reckless motorist is stopped by a police officer.

Officer of the law "Sir Are you aware of how poorly you were changing lanes?"

I'm sorry, officer, but I'm inebriated.

"That's not a good justification to allow your boyfriend drive the automobile," the policeman said.

63.

Policeman: "Where were you on the murderous night?"

"I was with a group of buddies," says Crow.

What would you name that bunch, policeman?

Crow: "I need an attorney."

64.

I observed a police officer stop a U-Haul today; it appeared like he was attempting to bust a move.

65.

When a police officer is found guilty of murder, what do you name them?

Nice beginning.

66.

A police officer stops a guy who rolls past a STOP sign.

"You did not stop at the stop sign, so I pulled you over. All you did was slow down."

"What's the difference between slowing down and stopping?"

The man is taken out of his automobile by the policeman, who then starts hitting him with a nightstick.

"Now tell me if you want me to slow down or stop."

67.

A drunken man leaves a pub.

A policeman approaches him outside and inquires, "What's your name, son?"

I'm Jesus Christ, the "drunk guy" responds.

The policeman declares, "You are not the Lord Jesus. Tell me your name."

The drunken man responds, "I'll offer proof. Observe me." He returns to the pub while being followed by the policeman.

The waiter shouts as they go in, "It's Jesus! Are you back once more?"

The inebriated man exclaims, "See?" as he turns to face a police officer.

68.

Why you are crying while writing me a ticket, the man asked.

"There is a moving violation," said the policeman.

69.

"A police officer pulled me up as I was performing donuts in my automobile. You're probably wondering, who gives their dog the name Donuts."

70.

Me: "How many times you get back up matters more than how many times you fall."

"That's not how sobriety tests operate," said the policeman.

BEST SHORT POLICE JOKES

1.

What do a DJ and a police officer have in common?

Both of them order inebriated people to raise their hands.

2.

Why are cemeteries surrounded by a gate?

As everyone is clamoring to enter!

3.

Was the policeman dozing off at work?

He was a covert agent.

4.

Why do all police officers have foul farts?

Since they are pigs!

5.

What dines make the greatest police officers?

An animal police

6.

Why did the cops receive the coffee?

It was robbed.

7.

The policeman attended the baseball game for what reason?

After he learned that a base had been taken!

8.

Why is a traffic officer the world's strongest man?

Because he can halt a 10-ton truck with the wave of a hand!

9.

Police were notified about a guy riding his bike around a neighborhood while shouting racist epithets.

He told them he was looking for his dog, Snickers, when they arrested him.

10.

Have you heard the story of the burglar who stole a lamp?

He received a relatively mild punishment.

11.

An airman on leave who had been ticketed for speeding sought to convince the officer not to write him a penalty.

Would it matter if I told you I'm in the Air Force? he enquired.

"Yes, but only if you were driving an airplane," the policeman said.

12.

Why didn't the cops arrive at Capitol Hill earlier today?

Because they needed to first change at home.

13.

What prompted the NYPD to attend the Mets game? They learned that bases were being stolen.

14.

Twenty police officers and one fire engine respond to a call. What took place?

Burning down was Dunkin' Donuts.

15.

Police: "Madam, how did your husband pass away?"

Spouse: poison (hysterically crying)

But the police saw that he was covered with bruises.

Wife: I'm aware. He was reluctant to accept it.

16.

Upon receiving a speeding ticket from a police officer, a lady questions why she wasn't initially given a warning. "Ma'am, there are warnings placed up and down this route," the officer continues. A 65 mph speed limit is posted.

17.

Do you too receive the majority of your pay in bribery, the Russian asks?

What exactly are "bribes"?

Somali: "What does 'salary' mean?

18.

What do you call a prison-escapee clairvoyant? A medium-sized.

19.

Why did the turkey be arrested by the police? They had a sneaking suspicion.

20.

Because a bottle of water was requested in three states, a police officer detained it. Gas, liquid, and solid.

21.

What is the name of the riot police in Germany? Control of the sour kraut

22.

According to the police, I "assaulted" a man with a sheet of sandpaper.

But I barely slightly roughed him up.

23.

"The cops are attempting to prove that I physically hurt a man with a piece of sandpaper. I only roughed him up a little."

24.

The erasure of people's criminal records was discovered by the police. For a first offender, they claimed he was a true pro.

25.

Who is the most well-known lawn investigator? Sleuth gnomes.

26.

What do you respond when your friend requests that you tell them a funny police joke? "Freeze!"

27.

What was spoken during the policeman's dinner?

In the name of the law, Irish stew

28.

What do you call a policeman who is blonde? A good policeman!

29.

What kind of insects enlist? The police

30.

Why do police officers sing so much? They never miss a beat!

REDDIT POLICE JOKE:

1.

What transpired after the wig was taken? Officers searched the area!

2.

What occurs when a car is stolen? You are put in a vehicle!

3.

A dog walker's pups were stolen, and the police had no leads!

4.

Which police division exterminates flies? The SWAT group!

5.

Why was the duvet detained by the police? They were aware that it was hiding something!

6.

What does a frog employ as a deterrent to thieves? An iris padlock!

7.

After dusting Chris Rocks' face following the performance, what did the cops discover?

Clean Prince

8

"I just saw a police car collide with a fire truck in the middle of town. I had planned to call for an ambulance, but doing so may have been risky."

9.

"Went to a rock festival and was detained for providing the cops with marijuana. The was a

10

Why did the cops allow Van Gogh to enter?

He had a reliable alibi. Stinging action."

11.

Why the police train bomb dogs to operate at airports is beyond my comprehension. They all cut the wrong wire because they are colorblind.

12.

Did Santa buy you that, a policeman on a horse asks a little girl on a bike.

Yes, the little girl answers. She is given a $5 fine and is told to "suggest him to put a reflector light on it next year."

The young child remarks, "Nice horse you've got there, did Santa bring you that?" as she raises her eyes to the policeman.

He absolutely did, the policeman responds with a chuckle. The young girl responds, "Well, tell Santa that his organ goes under the horse, not on top of it, next year!"

13.

A senior couple is stopped and...

"May I see your license and registration, sir?" said the female police officer.

Old man: "What the hell did she say?"

"She needs to see your license and registration, honey," said the elderly woman.

The senior police officer receives it from the elderly guy, and...

A female police officer "I see you're a New Yorker. The worst boyfriend I've ever had was a New Yorker who I once had."

Old man: "What the hell did she say?"

"Nothing, honey, she believes she used to know you," said the elderly wife.

14.

A policeman approaches a battered and bloody man outside of a bar. He inquires as to what transpired, and the guy replies as follows; "As I wait for my drink after entering the bar and sitting down, I overhear two enormous women speaking in an odd dialect. Are you two ladies from Ireland, I ask them. One of them laughs and says, "It's Wales," to me. I thus re-ask, "Are you two whales from Ireland?" That's pretty much all I can recall."

15.

A pig with wings enters a pub. The bartender is shocked and says: "Food from another restaurant cannot be brought in here! Even if you're a police officer!"

16.

An Australian travels to America for vacation. A police officer spots him driving on the wrong side of the road as he travels in his rental automobile. Do you realize you're driving on the wrong side of the road!? He exclaims as he pulls him over. Oh, I'm from Australia, the Australian replies. "Well, did you come here to die!?" the officer asks. No, the Australian responds. I arrived here yesterday.

17

"I once witnessed a woman filling up her automobile at a petrol station while smoking a cigarette. As soon as she yanked the nozzle out, gas flew everywhere and her arm instantly burst into flames. When she began to wave it about, a police officer noticed her and fatally shot her. She was displaying an unauthorized weapon."

18.

What caused the peanut to dial 911? It was a salty conclusion!

19.

A military, a police officer, and a politician face three burglars after they break into a building. The two stab each other to death when the politician orders the soldier to execute Burglar #1. The two then beat each other senseless before the politician orders the policeman to arrest Burglar #2. After that, the politician approaches Burglar #3 and says "I just quadrupled your part of the booty, saved your life, and secured your freedom. 20%, in my opinion, is a reasonable reduction."


PUNS AND JOKES BY POLICE ARE SO FUNNY:

1.

Last night, the ideal crime was committed. All the restrooms were taken after a break-in at the police station. Police claim they have no evidence.

2.

When a female police officer picks up a guitar, what do you call her? She-riff.

3.

Why did the policeman have such a foul smell? He was working.

4.

I see that your eyes are bloodshot, officer. Have you have any alcohol?

"I saw your eyes are glazed over," the driver said. Have you recently consumed donuts?

5.

Are you aware that the celery was detained? He was accused of stalking.

6.

Do you know how fast you were travelling, the officer asked?

Driver: "Shouldn't you be telling me?

7

During a fight, I tossed a 9V Duracell at my wife.

Police detained me for violence but were unable to file charges.

8.

Cop: "I estimated that you were at least 55 when I observed you driving down the road."

Driver: "Officer, you're mistaken. I only appear that elderly because of my headgear.

9.

Why did you park here, officer? The sign reads, "Fine for parking," I said.

10.

What is the prison's policy on self-service coffee mugs? fie.

11.

Why was the cap detained? It served as a marker's cover.

12.

Do you understand why I pulled you over, officer?

13.

What does a frog employ as a deterrent to thieves? A lock with lilies.

14.

I thought I said I never wanted to see you in here again, the judge remarked.

Criminal: "I continued trying to get the arresting officer to hear me, but he wouldn't."

15.

I placed first in a race and received an iPhone 13. The phone's owner and police officers are the other two rivals.

16.

The thief was wearing blue gloves, why? He didn't want to get busted for his crimes.

17.

Can I park here, please?"

Cop: "No." What about all these other automobiles, the man said. They didn't ask, says the cop.

18.

Why was the duvet detained by the police? They were aware that it was hiding something!

19.

How do you welcome a police officer when you meet them?

20.

A guy who pretended to be a helium balloon was detained yesterday. After holding him for a bit, the cops released him.

21.

Why did the police issue a ticket to the ghost? It lacked a license to haunt.

22.

Please knock. Anyone there? Dishes. Dishes, who? The cops with dishes. Lean in!

23.

People have said I light up a room.

The claim it was an arson, and those individuals are "witnesses."

24.

What television program does the police department investigate garden gnome crimes on?

Law and order

25.

Some people use se, while others clean the streets.

26.

Where do you think you're going, officer?

Donut store, officer, said the driver. At eighty miles per hour? Driver: "I made sure I arrived before you so there would still be donuts available for purchase."

27.

A miner was stopped by a policeman.

Policeman: What are you doing, who's automobile is this, and where are you going?

The miner

28.

Why the cat was issued a fine? Iglittereded.

29.

Why was the police officer asleep?

He worked as a covert officer.

30.

A police officer pulls up a driver for speeding and sees the man is missing his prescription glasses.

I have to write you a ticket for not having your spectacles on, officer. I have contacts, officer, says the driver. I don't care who you know, you're still getting a ticket, said the officer.

31.

How come the coffee dialed 911? It was stolen.

32.

When the remote control that beat up his wife was taken into custody, what did the policeman say?

'I use batteries to charge you.

33.

I was stopped by a policeman who said, "Papers."

"Scissors," I said. I triumph!" and sped off. Given that he has been following me for approximately 45 minutes, I assume he wants another fight.

34.

Did you hear the Energizer bunny was taken into custody? He was battery-charged.

35.

At closing time, an officer witnesses a guy leaving a pub and entering his automobile. He stops the man after seeing some reckless driving.

Where are you going at this hour of the night, the officer queries the motorist? I'm headed to a lecture about alcohol misuse and its effects on the body, as well as smoking and staying out late, the man responds. Who would deliver that type of sermon at this time of night, the officer wonders. "My wife," the man replies.

36.

Someone took the police station's restrooms.

Police have no evidence to work with.

37.

What transpires when a policeman retires to bed?

He goes undercover as a police officer.

38.

Do you realize how fast you were traveling, officer?

Sorry, I was simply trying to catch up with traffic, the driver said. There isn't any traffic, officer. This road is deserted. Driver: "I'm telling you that because I'm far behind."

39.

Why is a traffic officer the world's strongest man?

Considering that he can stop a 10-ton vehicle by only raising his hand!

40.

Have you heard the story of the two nutcases who wandered through a seedy neighborhood?

One person was abused.

JOKES WITH A POLICE OFFICER:

1.

Why did the cookie go to the hospital?

Because he was miserable

2.

Why did her lover be locked up by the sheriff?

He took her affections.

3.

Last night, a policeman pulled me over.

I'll follow you to the closest police station, said the officer. "What for?" I ask. Policeman: "I've lost the route." Thomas Cooper

4.

"How high are you, officer?" Driver: "No, officer, it's just a hello."

5.

Why did the turkey be arrested by the police? They had a sneaking suspicion.

6.

I cannot get any radio signal.

7.

The air outdoors has a stench of arrest warrants and revoked licenses.

8.

Because a bottle of water was requested in three states, a police officer detained it. Gas, liquid, and solid.

9.

Like Lays potato chips, LED lights are addictive.

10.

Today, pizza often arrives at your door before the cops.

11.

A female police officer stopped a lady who was driving too quickly. She had to show the officer her driver's license. She got angrier and angrier as she rummaged through her handbag. What does it resemble, the lady enquired. It's square, and it has your photo on it, the policewoman retorted. The motorist eventually pulled out a square mirror from her purse, examined it, and gave it to the officer. She said, "This is it. You can leave now, the officer responded after taking a peek in the mirror. I had no idea you were a police officer.

12.

A police officer observed a graffiti artist writing in large letters on a police station.

He regarded the artwork and remarked, "Now that is brave," before handcuffing the artist.

13.

If you haven't seen your wife smile her sexiest at a traffic officer, you haven't seen her.

14.

According to American police, 9/11 will never be forgotten. Given that it is your phone number, I would imagine it to be rather difficult.

15.

Do the police inform the mime that he has the right to stay quiet if he is arrested?

16.

A Montana police officer will stop you because he is lonely.

17.

Police officer to suspect: "Did you kill this man?"

Preparation: "No, he passed away naturally."
Policeman: "He was shot!" Right, he was killed by a gunshot. Lead, the material used to make bullets, is mined. The earth is a component of nature. So he passed away from natural causes. I assumed you were the local policeman, sheesh.

18.

Preparing cop: "Where do you live?"

With my parents, please. Where do your folks reside, policeman? Say "With me." Police: "Where do all of you live?" Together, prepare. Where is your residence, officer? "Near my neighbor's house," in preparation. Where is your neighbor's residence, officer? If I told you anything, would you trust me? Officer: "Tell me." "Next to my house," you say.

19.

The entire time the guy was berating me, all I could think was, "I should trim my bangs," which is why I disagree that police officers should wear mirror sunglasses.

20.

Who collaborates with the grammar enforcers? Officers of the law.

21.

The finest auto safety feature is a police officer in the rearview mirror.

22.

What kind of tag is a police officer's preferred one? Frost tag.

23.

How are individuals greeted by police? I'm happy to meet you!

24.

The amount of time a traffic control officer is monitoring a roadway correlates with an increase in traffic congestion.

CRAZY COPS JOKE

1.

Who is the female police officer who is currently strumming an electric guitar called? The she-riff is who she is!

2.

What should I do with this speeding ticket? I asked him when the cops stopped me for speeding. The policeman said, "Save it. A bicycle is yours after you have four of them."

3.

Did the cops seize the thief who was merely robbing the police cars of their wheels? No, they haven't yet captured him, but they're working nonstop to do so!

4.

Why did the turkey down the road be arrested by the police? Because there were suspicions of wrongdoing.

5.

What do you name the policeman who focuses on crimes using computers? You refer to the policeman as a troubleshooter.

6.

When do you think a police officer will be found dozing off while on duty? Who is the world's toughest police officer while they are undercover? The strongest police officer in the world is a traffic officer because he has the ability to halt even the largest trucks with a simple hand wave.

7.

A police officer's nightstick contains more legal authority than a Supreme Court ruling.

8.

Why did the cops detain the energizer bunny? Because a battery was used to charge it!

9.

What transpired to the burglar who was apprehended by the police after stealing a priceless lamp? The thief received a mild punishment!

10.

What sort of topping does a cop detest on his toast in the morning? a gridlock.

11.

What took place after the policeman stopped the famous person for driving while intoxicated? He was in the police officer's selfie.

12.

Why do most volleyball players make excellent law enforcement officials? Because they are skilled in protecting and serving!

13.

Why did the police like the prospect of apprehending the victor of the quickest dog-eating contest? Because the victor had been driving too fast.

14.

Try not to run through a tunnel, then onto a little seesaw, then leap through a flaming hoop while being pursued by a police dog; they are trained for that!

15.

To which team was the officer sent when he proved his fly-catching prowess? The SWAT squad received the cop's assignment.

16.

When all the real estate board games vanished from his business, who did the toy store owner call? He dialed the Mono-Police number right away.

17.

When the police detained the optometrist for murder, what did he say? "Officer, I'm being accused of killing someone!"

18.

Who is the name of the band that the police play in their cars? They take in "The Police."

19.

Why did the detectives from the police station erect offices all along the beach? Because they anticipated a wave of crime.

20.

Why did the police wrongfully terminate the sketch artist's employment? A instance of mistaken identity had occurred.

21.

What is the name of the special police division that determines whether or not everyone is properly attired? They are known as the "Fashion Police."

22.

What is the most typical method a police officer will welcome another police officer when they cross paths? They exclaim, "Policed to meet and converse with you!" to one another.

23.

Which day of the week is the only one when an undercover police officer is wearing a uniform? Today is the officer's off-duty day.

CRINGY POLICE JOKES:

1.

Why was the celery taken into custody by the policeman? It was due to the stalking accusation against him.

2.

Which location in town is the only one with round-the-clock police protection from burglars and thieves? Your local doughnut store.

3.

Why did the policeman charge the ghost and take him into custody? Mostly because the ghost was operating without a valid haunting permit.

4.

What do you do when a police officer pulls you over to write you a ticket and requests paper? You cut it up with scissors and then you drive away!

5.

Did the policeman detain the elderly woman who shot someone because she stepped on a section of the floor she had recently mopped? Because the floor was still wet, the officer decided against arresting her.

6.

Why did the policeman pull over a bottle of water when it was moving down the street? Because it was required in all three of its states—gas, solid, and liquid—at the same time.

7.

What do you say when a state trooper or police officer works overtime? You mention that he's taking copper nitrate.

8.

Why were so many investigators and police officers at the baseball game? Because the base had been reported as stolen.

9.

Why was the police officer's lover imprisoned? Due to the fact that she stole the officer's heart.

10.

Why did the cops not apprehend the robber who was sporting blue gloves? Because they were unable to capture him in the act!

11.

Which gardening program do the various police forces throughout the world prefer to watch? They adore the television program "Lawn Order"!

12.

When a business was on fire, why did so many police cars and just one fire engine arrive? It was because a doughnut store was involved in the fire.

13.

Why did the coffee make such an early morning police call? He called to report being robbed!

14.

The elderly woman who had misplaced her wig in the area was assured what by the police. They promised to search the region.

15.

Why did the officer stop the automobile that was covered in odd paints and sketches in various colors? Because this was a very graphic offense.

16.

Why was the officer detained on grounds of cannibalism? Because he was observed questioning each suspect.

17.

Why do you contact a police officer who is proficient in flight? The chopper

18.

Why did the bicycle police let the robbers siphon fuel from the pump without intervening? Because they didn't have fuel!

19.

What transpired when the drummer of a rock band chose to enroll in the police academy? As a beat cop after graduation.

20.

Why did the doctor be arrested by the police when he was examining a patient? Considering that he was charged with taking the patient's pulse!

21.

What condition causes someone to become unwell only by observing a police car following them?

You claim that the individual has cop-sick shock syndrome.

22.

When the officer questioned the suspect about what he was doing between five and six, what did he say? The suspect retorted that he was a preschooler at the time.

23.

Why don't cows ever become successful police officers? As a result of their abhorrence of participating in a steak-out while on duty!

24.

Why were bugs permitted to join the ranks of state troopers? Because they are a crucial component of the police.

25.

What justification was offered when the space police detained a star without a reason? Because it was a shooting star, the police officer alerted the media that the arrest had been made.

26.

Why was the renowned sculptor chosen to join the police force? Owing to the sculptor's prowess in creating busts.

27.

The hardback book wanted to join the police force for what reason? Because he was really motivated to become a covert agent.

KNOCK-KNOCK POLICE JOKES:
Here are a few practical jokes that are ideal for police humor. You never know when the jokes police could show up at your front door to arrest you if you don't think them humorous.

1.

Please knock! Anyone there? Police.

Whose police? Please open the door quickly!

2.

Please knock! Who are they?

My name is. Me who?

The crocodile cop!

You are the investigator, I see.

3.

Please knock!

Who are they? We are it. Us who?

FB...Facebook? FBI, let me in!

## POLICE HUMOR FOR KIDS:

1.

How many police officers are required to install a light bulb?

None, please. The thing surrenders.

2.

I've never had a drug issue... I've encountered issues with the cops.

3.

When I once enquired as to the distance to the subway, a police officer replied, "I don't know, no one has ever reached it."

4.

I enjoy how the phrase "To protect and serve" appears in quotes on police cars, as if they were making a sarcastic statement.

5.

What does a frog employ to keep robbers' lily pads at bay?

6.

According to a new police research, running increases your risk of being shot by a fat officer.

7.

Tonight the cops showed up at my house with a photo of my wife.

Is this your wife, sir? They questioned. I reacted shocked and said "Yes."

I'm afraid it appears like she was struck by a bus, they stated.

I acknowledged that, but she has a great personality, I said.

8.

At the police station, what kind of pictures do you take? A cellular fi!

9.

What was the policeman's comment to his stomach?

You're wearing a vest,

10.

Why did the police fine the cat? It was filthy!

11.

What prompted the peanut to dial 911? A SALT was applied!

12.

What do you call a traveling psychic? A medium-sized medium!

13.

What do you get when you cross a police officer with a tennis player? Someone who looks out for and defends!

14.

Why was the police called by the coffee? It was robbed!

15.

What do you call a policeman who is blonde? A decent policeman!

16.

Why was the pet store searched by the police? They were on the lookout for the cat thief!

17.

Who is the garden's most well-known detective? Detective Gnomes!

18.

What may seize you, has keys, and a screen? A PC!

19.

Why was the celery detained by the police? The accusation was stalking!

20.

What made the officer detain her husband? He stole her heart, that's why!

21.

Why was the fish and chips detained by the police? Salt and batteries, ah!

22.

What do you do when a police officer is keeping an eye on cows? Steak night!

23.

What kind of insects enlist? The police

24.

What led to the ghost's arrest? It lacked a license to haunt!

25.

What transpired after the wig was taken? Officers searched the area!

26.

Why did the police officer grill out? Interviewing the suspects was going on!

27.

We do police travel? In a heli-cop-ter!

28.

What happens when you steal a vehicle? You get in-car-cerated!

29.

Someone stole some dogs from a dog walker...The police have no leads!

30.

Which police unit gets rid of flies? The SWAT team!

31.

My wife has begged me to stop making police related puns...

I said ok... I will give it arrest.

32.

What did the policeman say to the man's navel? You're wearing a vest.

33.

The vampire joined the police force for what reason?

To enable him to learn how to set a stake out

34.

When a policeman asked me where I was between the ages of 5 and 6, he seemed annoyed when I replied kindergarten.

Printed in Great Britain
by Amazon